Situation Report N

MISSION TO MUSLIMS IN GERMANY

A Case Study of the "Orientdienst" - the

Major Mission Organization

Ahmad von Denffer

The Islamic Foundation

© The Islamic Foundation 1980/1400 A.H.
Reprinted New Format 1985/1406 A.H.

ISBN 0 86037 165 4

Published by:

The Islamic Foundation
223, London Road
Leicester LE2 1ZE

Printed in England by:
JOSEPH BALL (Printers) LTD.,
72 Cannock Street,
Leicester
Tel: (0533) 740880

CONTENTS

Introduction   5

I   The Mission Field: Immigrant Muslims in Germany   7

II   The Missionary's Understanding of Islam   12

III   The Roots and Role of "Orientdienst"   13

IV   Major Activities of the Organization   21

V   A Special Approach: Through Children to Parents   29

VI   "Orientdienst" Literature   33

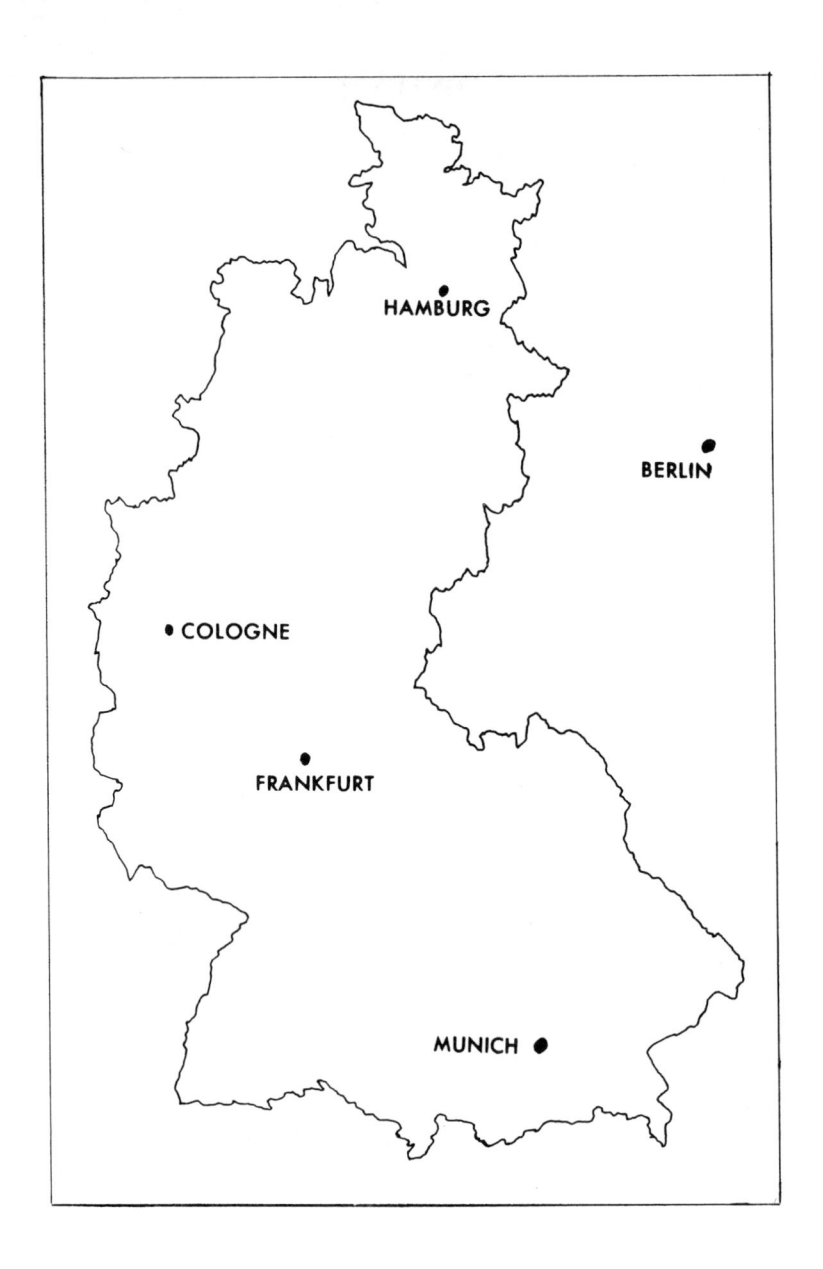

WEST GERMANY

INTRODUCTION

Mission to Muslims is generally understood to mean the efforts by some European or American Christian missionaries travelling to Muslim lands to convert Muslims to Christianity. Recent developments have, however, brought millions of Muslims to the West, and today mission to Muslims takes place not only in the Orient, but also in the heart of the West itself.

The following report is an account of such missionary work among Muslims in the West. It is a case study of the mission organization "Orientdienst", which is a free cooperative association of Protestant mission organizations aiming to reach those foreigners in the Federal Republic of Germany who come from the lands of Islam, i.e. especially the Turks. Muslims in Germany number perhaps about 1.5 million and the majority of them are immigrants from Turkey. Their socio-economic position and their legal status are weak and their religion, i.e. Islam, has not been officially recognized by the government as a religious body. This makes social work and care among Muslims very necessary, and hence many openings for missionary work do exist.

In this study, both the historical origins as well as the nature of the work by "Orientdienst" are analysed. There are a number of similarities between the work of German missionaries in Egypt, who combined medical care with literature evangelism, and the work of "Orientdienst", now engaged in social care and literature evangelism. The main areas in which the missionaries work are: production and distribution of literature, gatherings, radio broadcasts, children's programmes, correspondence, contacts with organized Muslim groups.

A special approach of the missionaries is also outlined. They aim at reaching the parents by way of the children, who are being taken care of by the missionaries in the afternoons. Muslim parents, usually both husband and wife, working in factories appreciate any assistance with regard to their children and, naturally, whatever influence the missionaries gain upon the children will show some effect on the family as a whole in one way or another.

Finally, a brief description of the literature produced by "Orientdienst" is also included in this report. Although "Orientdienst" is not the sole organization doing missionary work among Muslims in Germany, it is the most prominent Protestant organization of its kind and its work does have strong similarities with approaches of similar organizations in other European countries, such as France, the Netherlands, the U.K. and even outside Europe, as in the U.S. and Canada.

It is hoped that this case study will serve as an eye-opener to Muslims generally and in particular to those Muslims who are now in a position to assist those of their brothers who, due to a weak socio-economic and legal position, are very much exposed to the work of Christian missionaries in the West.

I
THE MISSION FIELD: IMMIGRANT MUSLIMS IN GERMANY

1. General

With the influx of more than one million Muslim immigrant labourers and their families from Turkey into Germany during the 1960s, Christians and the Christian churches and organizations in Germany were for the first time in history confronted with the presence of a large number of Muslims in their own country. Previously, almost all contacts between Christians and Muslims had been in the lands of Islam.

During the 19th century, missionaries had encountered Muslims in some of the African territories that the short-lived German Empire had attempted to colonize before World War I. Both East African and West African Muslim peoples and societies were among the objects of studies in German academic institutions and universities. For a short while Swahili and Hausa became popular as languages to be acquired by missionaries-to-be.

While, due to political circumstances, the emphasis had thus been on Islam in Africa, a number of mission organizations had also been operating in other parts of the Muslim world. Among them were some groups in the then Dutch East Indies, along with the Dutch Protestant churches, others in various parts of the Ottoman Empire, and in the Anglo-Egyptian Sudan, as well as in Egypt itself.

Orientdienst, the organization selected for the study to examine the nature and extent of missions to Muslims in Germany and described in the following pages, has its roots in one of those 19th-century missionary organizations which were taking up missionary work in Egypt and the Sudan then, namely the "Sudan Pioneer Mission". Some of the heritage of this mission organization is still to be met up with in the actual work of the Orientdienst, as will be apparent later.

The situation in which the churches and missionary organizations found themselves within Germany in the

1960s was different from all the past encounters with Muslims. Nevertheless, the churches in Germany, in their missions to the large number of immigrant Muslims, turned to the same clergy and staff who had some previous relation and experience with work among Muslims, because of their membership of the missionary organizations that had gone out to the Muslim countries in the last century, and are still operating there even today.[1]

2. Demographic Data [2]

The total population of Germany in 1970 (the latest census) was 60,650,000, out of which 47% were Protestants, 44.6% Roman Catholics, 0.1% Jews and 1.3% others. Since Islam is not officially recognized as a religion in Germany, Muslims are counted as "others".

A count of citizens of countries with a Muslim majority residing in Germany indicates the approximate number of Muslims in this country as 1,202,183. Most of them come from Turkey (27% of all foreigners), Morocco (0.7%), Iran (0.5%), Tunisia (0.4%) and other places.

It is difficult to distinguish between migrant and indigenous Muslims, since no data is available. The number of indigenous Muslims, however, must be very insignificant. Data given by Abdullah/Mildenberger [3] does not seem to be right in the light of official statistics giving the number of persons that came from some major Muslim countries and acquired German citizenship as 1,282 in 1974 and 855 in 1975.

---

1. See the official publication by the Protestant Church of Germany on encounter with Muslims: 'Muslime - unsere Nachbarn', Frankfurt, 1977, to which the Director of Orientdienst contributed substantially.
2. For details see: Denffer, A.v.: 'Survey of Muslims in Europe: Germany (June 1978), unpublished.
3. Moslems unter uns. Situation, Herausforderung, Gesprach Stuttgart 1974.

3. **Legal Problems**

Although West Germany's "Grundgesetz" provides for freedom of worship and religion, Islam and Muslims face a number of problems both legal and social. Legal problems are mainly two.

Firstly, Islam does not officially exist in Germany. All attempts to have the Muslim community legally recognized by the Government as a religious body have so far failed. German law requires that a religious group which wishes to be officially recognized as such - and only this "recognition" gives a legal status to its members - must have a "sufficient number" of adherents residing permanently in Germany. While nobody can question the figures of Muslims present in Germany, the Government authorities contend that the majority of Muslims in Germany are not permanent residents and therefore recognition cannot be granted. Statistics, however, reveal that many more Muslims than, for example, Jews are now permanently residing in Germany, and Judaism is of course officially recognized. Attempts to gain recognition have also failed partly due to the lack of co-operation among the Muslim associations who have not been strong enough to put forward their case jointly.

Secondly, Muslims in Germany face major obstacles due to Germany's law for foreigners, which covers most of the Muslims who came as immigrant labourers. While during the period of economic growth after World War II more than a million Turkish labourers were imported by German factories, the law remained as it was before. Under this law, the residence permits are granted for a period of one year in most cases and labour permits are issued only for a single employment. A man who wants to change his job is at the mercy of the local authorities, who decide whether to give another labour permit or not. Where the two basic conditions, residence and labour, are handled almost arbitrarily, the legal position of the individuals affected is indeed very weak. The fact that at the same time their religious creed is not officially recognized only adds to that weak position.

4. Social Problems

While all immigrants face various problems, the Turkish Muslims in Germany, compared to the Italians, Spanish, Greek etc., face additional difficulties due to their religion and culture. Housing has been and still is a main problem for all immigrant labourers in Germany, but the worst places are rented out to the Turkish for the highest rents. Food and diet are also a major problem. Pork is even more common in Germany than in other European countries. Foodstuffs normally do not have their ingredients printed on the labels. Halal meat is hard to get, since slaughtering can be done only in special slaughterhouses, approved by the local authorities.

The Muslim children going to German schools are at a considerable disadvantage as compared to their classmates. About two-thirds of them at present do not even obtain the lowest qualification possible, i.e. a school leaver's certificate.

5. Christian-Muslim Relations

Hardly any relations exist between Christians and Muslims, although some of the church organizations make considerable noise about their schemes, programmes and activities. Both Protestant and Catholic organizations have formed committees to look into the Muslim affairs, but the Muslim participation is insignificant and whosoever participated in the past was selected on the basis of his utility for the churches rather than for the Muslims.

The main Catholic institution is the OKNI (Ecumenical Contact Centre for Non-Christians) in Cologne, operating on a local level. Recently OKNI decided to start a documentation centre for Christian-Muslim relations.

Initially Protestants for some time had their centre of activities at the EZW (Protestant Centre for Questions of Ideologies) in Stuttgart. However, interest somewhat decreased, and a study group on Islam and Muslims was then formed in Frankfurt. A joint committee by the churches wishing to concentrate on the problems of Muslim immigrant labourers is now operating, since about three years ago, and has also involved some Muslims. However, no results have so far come out for the benefit of Muslims. They will continue to have their problems since they are immigrants, and there are no serious efforts to change their lot.

A number of attempts by genuine Muslim community workers to establish relations with some of the above mentioned church bodies have been turned down by them with the co-operation of such Muslims as they have themselves selected for "representing" Muslims. Thus Christian-Muslim relations on a wider than individual basis hardly exist.

Christian mission to Muslims has to be seen against this background. Muslims in Germany are an economically, politically, socially and culturally extremely weak minority, and thus present a fertile "mission field" for Christian mission.

II

THE MISSIONARY'S UNDERSTANDING OF ISLAM

As commonly found in Christian and especially evangelical circles, Islam is simply understood as an after-Christ phenomenon and consequently as completely wrong and false.

"Generally speaking, one may understand Islam as an imitation of Christianity. By having many common traits with Christian belief, and by even giving Jesus an important position, Islam makes its adherents immune to the true gospel. It is in this imitating falsification where the anti-Christian character of Islam lies. The enemy of God is not only seducer, falsificator (see I Mos. 30), but also the sinister imitator of God."[1]

This radically anti-Islamic position is the basis which justifies an aggressive missionary approach to Muslims, for where even common traits are explained as being the exact opposite of what one usually understands by that very concept,[2] there can be no room for co-existence. It is in this context that one should consider the relationship between the evangelical groups and other factions of Christianity. Although there is no doubt that opinions differ between all of them on a number of issues, the aggressiveness of the evangelicals is something which the majority groups in Christianity also employ to further their own ends, if they feel the evangelicals can be of use. This is well illustrated in the case of the latest guidelines for Protestant Christians on encounter with Muslims in Germany, published in 1977 by the EKD.[3] The publication includes contributions by a number of writers, among whom the head of Orientdienst is also to be found.

1. *Zeugnis und Dienst* 1/76, p.14
2. Common traits are usually something that should encourage understanding and perhaps even fruitful exchange of views, while in this case they are said to be fabrications and the very basis of the anti-Christian character of Islam, i.e. factors that prevent understanding and exchange.
3. i.e. Protestant Church of Germany. The full title of the brochure is "Muslime unsere Nachbarn".

III

ORIENTDIENST: HISTORICAL BACKGROUND

1. General

We have already indicated that we intend to study Orientdienst as a typical organization to examine the nature and extent of Missions to Muslims. To better understand Orientdienst in Germany, it is necessary to understand the Protestant Mission in Upper Egypt (EMO), which operates in Egypt and Tunisia. For there are a number of similarities between Orientdienst and EMO, mainly because the staff of Orientdienst comes partly from EMO.

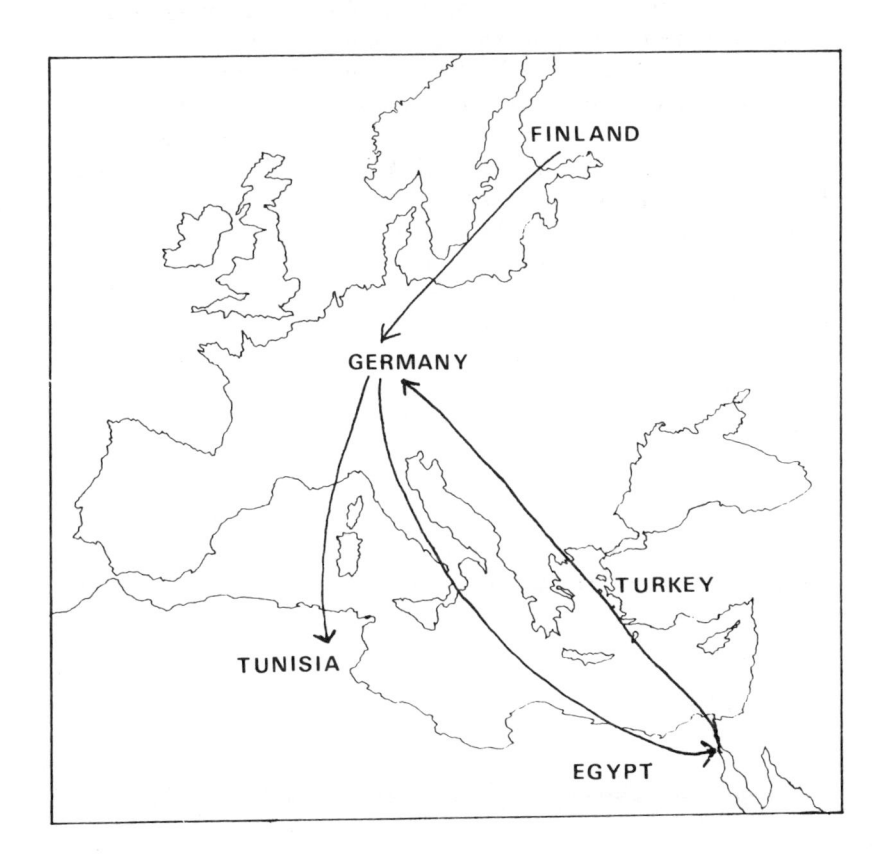

2. Protestant Mission in Upper Egypt

The EMO was founded in the year 1900, after the Upper Nile region had become more prominent in the day to day affairs of Europeans since the Mahdi struggle against the British in the Sudan. When in 1901 a piece of land was bought in Aswan (Egypt) on which the missionary station was erected soon afterwards, a good number of supporters could be won in both Germany and Switzerland. The official headquarters of EMO, originally named as Sudan Pioneer Mission, was set up in Wiesbaden, Germany. Between 1904 and 1915 the efforts of the mission organization which, from the very beginning, had involved a Nubian Christian and made him a full-time employee of the mission in Aswan, concentrated on medical and educational work, while literature mission was also pursued. A small clinic was set up before 1914 in Aswan, and medical staff concentrated on eye diseases, which are most common in this area. The radius of impact for the missionaries was enlarged first up to a distance of 40 km and reached about 100 km around Aswan in 1939.

Due to World War I, the European involvement in mission in that part of the world suffered considerably and organized work was discontinued after 1915. Also, between 1939 and 1950, no German staff were allowed in Egypt. However, during World War II, a number of Swiss missionaries kept up the work and were later rejoined by missionaries from Germany. Soon afterwards, the EMO work in Egypt continued on its former lines: "A number of outposts had been established, and the mission now described its activity as "evangelization by preaching and distribution of literature in connection with medical care on the three stations, Aswan, Darsu and Dakke and the surrounding areas." [1]

---

1. *Zeugnis und Dienst*, Sondernummer 5 (October 1975).

3. **Medical Mission**

Both the 50-bed hospital in Aswan, run by EMO and the policlinic, provide ample opportunity for preaching and distribution of literature, and the linkage of evangelization with medical care exposes a great number of people to Christian mission, who would otherwise hardly be accessible. Medical care, however, opens many ways for approaching people and confronting them with Christianity's claims and teachings: "The preaching of the gospel is done in close connection with the healing activities. A sick person is, in most cases, open for an encouraging word. Language and thought of the Orientals are still filled with religious expressions and thoughts, so that it is not difficult to give him a support from the word of God. There is hardly any need to overcome a gap between secular vocabulary and religious language. However, in most cases, the conversation ends up in some futile exchanges. It is a gift from the Holy Spirit when an intensive discussion about the deeper issues of belief comes about. Due to its hectic character, the policlinic is not very suitable for such exchanges. Nevertheless, even here a number of situations occur, when Bible stories can be told and briefly related to the situation of the listener. Often in the rooms of the sick most fruitful discussions arise. It is an aim of the mission to present the word of God daily to each patient. More than 2,000 patients per year are given medical care. A much bigger number are going through the policlinic and in addition to that, many visitors hear the word of God from the wards. More than 90% of these people are Muslims." [2]

4. **Literature Mission**

Next to direct verbal preaching comes distribution of literature, which not only reaches the literate, but can

---

2. *Zeugnis und Dienst,* Sondernummer 5 (October 1975), p.18-19.

be read to a wide audience of illiterate persons, if a suitable surrounding can be arranged. Missionaries, therefore, see their literature as an essential tool for evangelization:

"The printed word is an essential aid for proclamation. Those patients and visitors able to read get Bible tracts, selections of Bible verses and other booklets. The more advanced reader may obtain a book from the well-stocked lending library of the missionary, which is also used by many people from Aswan and its surrounding area. This holds true also for the bookshop of the mission in Aswan, where Christian literature, presently available in Arabic, is offered. The literature work of the mission is done by some part-time assistants. While selling or borrowing books, often valuable discussions with Christians and Muslims arise." [3]

There are, of course, Sunday services held in both Arabic and German language, and preaching is undertaken on the occasion of various meetings, conferences or festive events. However, the link between medical care and presentation of the gospel is most prominent in the case of the outpost in Darau, where once per week a doctor sees patients, while on other days only out-patients are being received and attended by two nurses. Here the patients, coming not only from Darau but also from other places, hear a Bible story before being given medical attention.[4]

Afterwards they receive Christian literature and tracts to take home.

5. Orientdienst Role

The self-perception of Orientdienst is largely an outcome of its evangelical nature and its missionary tradition derived

---

3. *Zeugnis und Dienst im Orient*, Sondernummer 5, p.19-20.
4. Ibid., p.24: EMO understands that "due to the service of love most of the patients are open for the word of God".

from EMO. EMO justified its continuous presence in Egypt, in spite of the acknowledged development of medical facilities in this country,[5] on the grounds that the Coptic Church in Egypt never took up the missionary task amongst the Muslims. Orientdienst also sees itself, in contrast to the majority of established churches, some of which do not appreciate the work of Orientdienst[6] and others even openly criticize it,[7] in the same role. Thus, in both cases the picture that emerges has the following characteristics: a large number of Muslims, a Christian majority group, unable or unwilling to evangelize them, and a small team of missionaries, specializing in mission work among Muslims, by combining care with preaching and literature distribution.

However, there are some differences too. At the time when missionary work in Upper Egypt was taken up by EMO at the turn of the century, medical care was one of the most urgent needs of the Muslim population in that area, and it was a field in which missionaries could engage with full consent of the colonial authorities, who at times disfavoured other projects, especially in the domain of education. Thus, to engage in medical care was not only justifiable from a Christian viewpoint as service to the suffering and needy, but at the same time most suitable and opportune. But conditions in Germany are of an entirely different nature and medical care is easily available to anyone. Orientdienst therefore found a different field of service to which preaching and literature distribution could be linked. Due to a number of reasons, it was the social conditions of the majority of Muslims in Germany which provided such a field of service, once again suitable and opportune.

---

5. See *Zeugnis und Dienst*, Sondernummer 5 (October 1975) p.28; here it is also said: "... however, the diaconal aim of the medical work of the mission would not be guaranteed, if today the Western missionaries would fully withdraw."
6. See *EMO Nachrichten*, 4/76, pp.51-52.
7. See *Orientdienst Information* 54/79, pp. 6-7.

As the influx of Turkish immigrant labourers into Germany reached the one million mark, the Government sought the assistance of both religious and secular humanitarian organizations to cope with the immense difficulties that arose for the immigrants in the social sphere. Since immigrant labourers also came from a number of non-Muslim and from Christian countries, the following distribution of roles was implemented: the Roman Catholic Church with its bodies and organizations concentrated upon immigrants from traditionally Roman Catholic countries such as Italy, Spain and Portugal; the Protestant Churches, due to absence of immigrants from Protestant countries, accepted Greeks and Yugoslavs as their area of activities; while the secular welfare organizations were made to work upon the Turkish immigrants, to which neither Roman Catholics nor Protestants felt related in any way.

This distribution of roles was then responsible for the fact that no Christian church or organization was ever officially requested by the Government to involve itself with the affairs of Muslims in Germany. Whatever activities subsequently arose from within the churches were based upon decisions made within the churches, without any encouragement or discouragement from the Government. Generally speaking, the Government, however, appreciates any church activity that concentrates on the social sphere, since this eases the task and responsibilities of the political authorities.

Orientdienst, by relating its work among Muslims in Germany to issues arising from the social conditions of immigrants in Germany, chose a sensitive area which would allow many inlets for the missionary and enable him both to preach and distribute his literature, while the Government approves of the missionaries' involvement in social work without having any need to bother about the missionary task that he relates to his activities.

Other than these, the similarities between the understanding of the situation in Egypt and Germany are striking. Just as in Egypt the Coptic Church is blamed for not evangelizing the Muslims of that country, both the Protestant and the Roman Catholic Church have been accused by the evangelicals of neglecting the missionary task and of engaging in dialogue with Muslims instead of exposing them to more open forms of evangelism.. Orientdienst, like a missionary organization that works abroad, understands itself as the exceptional association that is faithful to the Christian task in the world, while the majority of Christians have turned away from it.

This is not the place to discuss the sectarian character of many of the missionary organizations, but it may be worthwhile to note that, while perceiving its own position as being outside of the ordinary Christian community, organizations such as Orientdienst, nevertheless, feel themselves somewhat related to the majority groups. At the same time, while the majority groups may have a number of differences with Orientdienst, they would always include them among those of the Christians who are engaged in active witnessing, although at times in ways not subscribed to by the majority. All this proves that the peculiar relationship between these various Christian groups enables most of them to claim that they are not directly engaged in evangelizing Muslims, while they can, at the same time, have a share in it by indirectly contributing in a number of ways.

An important way in which EMO directly supports the work of Orientdienst are the lectures, sermons, reports and visits to schools and other educational institutions undertaken by two or more of the staff members of EMO.[8] It should be noted, however, that, in a number of local Christian communities, the work of both EMO and Orientdienst are not always given full support. Consequently the missionary representatives understand their visits in such communities as a missionary task to enlarge support from the grass-root level:

---

8. See *EMO Nachrichten* 4/76, p.53.

"It would be completely wrong to understand the EMO travelling activities simply as collecting money for the missionary task. For that reason we believe that the considerable expenditure involved in this work is justified. As far as explanation of Islam and missionary encounter with Islam is concerned, EMO is perhaps the sole German Protestant missionary organization which carries this question into the parishes by a systematic travel service. The following figures reflect the service in the parishes:

"In 1975, EMO staff gave 47 sermons in church services, 139 Mission lectures ... 77 lectures in associations, 18 in free churches; 10 in Sunday Schools and children's services, 40 before confirmation classes, 11 in youth groups, 61 in school classes, 23 in women's circles, 2 in men's circles, 4 in old peoples' homes and 7 in other homes." [9]

---

9. *EMO Nachrichten* 4/76, pp.51-52.

IV

MAJOR ACTIVITIES OF ORIENTDIENST

1. Staff and Activities

A brief description of the Orientdienst by one of its new staff members gives the following picture of this organization and its activities:

"The Orientdienst is a free co-operative association Protestant mission organization. It aims particularly at the foreigners in the Federal Republic of Germany, that come from the area of Islam, i.e. the orientals and especially the Turks, who are the strongest group among them (approx. 1.4 million). These people so far have not heard the Gospel, or heard and seen it only insufficiently from Christians. And I believe if God has not only given us the missionary task but also placed the mission field right in front of our doors, it is disobedience and hidden egoism to reserve the glory of the living God to myself or ourselves instead of opening our hearts and houses to these people who need love, just as Jesus did.

"Of the ten full-time staff members of the Orientdienst, three are from Switzerland, four from Germany, two from Turkey and one with his family from Britain. There is a great deal of work, beginning with social services and contacts (translating at the authorities and doctors, helping with homework of school children etc.), children's programmes, bible study groups, preparing the Turkish programmes of the gospel broadcasts and the Turkish gospel calendar with all the letters and visits related to them, and information and bookstalls in various cities, conferences and meetings etc. An important branch of the Orientdienst, which may be most important for you, is the mail distribution of literature in foreign languages. Isn't it good that we can give to our foreign neighbour or colleague in addition to our friendliness and hospitality a tract or a radio programme in his own language, and also cassettes and books? Just now the time has come to distribute the Gospel calendars. This is not some kind of hidden advertising, but an aid for you, who just as myself do not speak Arabic, Serbian, Urdu, Hindi. For a tract is handed over quickly, but an intensive language training takes much longer." [1]

Special activities of Orientdienst for doing mission among Muslims are described in the following paragraphs. [2]

2. Community Gatherings

Muslim immigrant labourers have been invited to attend community gatherings in the afternoons or evenings in various places in West Germany. These invitations have been extended at regular intervals. A specific feature of these gatherings is that to free the Muslims from their isolation, both German and Muslim families are invited together. This aims at helping the Turkish Muslims understand that they have not been singled out to be exposed to the Gospel message, but that both Germans and Muslims do need the Gospel.

3. Radio Broadcasting

A number of broadcasts in both Turkish and Arabic have been produced and put on the air. From these broadcasts a great number of contacts develop and an increasing correspondence with Muslims is built up.

4. Children's Programmes

Some of the Orientdienst staff concentrate on attending regularly to the children of Muslim immigrant labourers. They look after them, helping with their homework after school, play with them and teach them handicrafts and "let them also share what is our greatest joy. These children, whose

---

1. *Orientdienst information* 53/1978, p.12.
2. From Orientdienst, Annual Report (Jahresbericht) 1978, in: *Orientdienst Information* 54/1979, p.2 ff.

Islamic education aims at submission and not at the amazement about God's love and mercy, are being led to an entirely new religious understanding. They experience that meeting Jesus makes you happy. You can talk to Him like to a friend. Prayer is genuine, natural conversation with God out of trust in Him. This is an entirely new experience for them".[3]

5. Literature

Work in the field of literature production and distribution took place in three languages, namely German, Turkish and Arabic. In co-operation with the "Sud-Ost-Europa Mission" a four-page newspaper in Turkish (named *Yasam*) has been published which enjoys wide circulation among the Turkish immigrant labourers.

---

3. Ibid., p.6.

A mobile bookstand of ORIENTDIENST in a city centre

Another major feature has been a calendar with gospel words for each day of the year. The number of calendars printed is about 10,000. About 1,800 of these calendars have been given free to Muslims from Turkey and other countries at present in German jails for various legal offences.

Newly published by Orientdienst during 1978 were the following books and booklets:
- *Suffering in Islamic Mysticism* (Das Leiden in der Islamischen Mystik).
- *The Muslim Jesus and We* (Der Moslemische Jesus und wir).
- *Islam in Indonesia* (Der Islam in Indonesien).
- *Certitude of Faith in Islam and the Gospel* (Glaubensgewissheit im Islam und im Evangelium).

In addition to this a number of the religious broadcasts have been made available on cassette.

Both printed and audio materials are being distributed at various occasions including the above-mentioned community gatherings. Some distribution also takes place by mail and mobile bookstands are operated in a number of German cities, to attract Muslims in the shopping areas of the city centres.

6. Correspondence

A great number of letters are addressed to Orientdienst requiring information and assistance of both a religious and pastoral nature, which is provided in many cases. No further details on the exact range and content of this correspondence is made available.

7. Contacts with Muslim Groups

At times invitations are being received and accepted to attend meetings of Muslim groups. During such occasions, which are particularly prominent in Ramadan, Muslims are open to discussion of both Islam's and Christianity's dogmas, and the Christian view of Jesus as Saviour for all mankind is being presented to the audience.

8. Some Major Orientdienst Programmes for 1979

1. Training camp for young Turkish Christians to be held from April 13-16, 1979 in Gernsheim (Bible studies, questions of concern, pastoral words and prayer in community).
2. Excursion into Eastern and Southern Turkey from April 7-22, 1979. (Samsun, Trabsun, Van Lake Van, Midiyat, Nardinete).
3. Training programme for witness among Muslims to be held from November 2-11, 1979 in Kaub (for details see below).
4. Orientdienst annual gathering in connection with the above training camp, to be held on November 3, 1979 in Kaub.

9. Advertising the Gospel Calendar

"Have you already thought about what you could possibly give to your Muslim neighbour as a Christmas present? We suggest to you the new Bible WallCalender. It is available in Arabic, Turkish and Urdu from Orientdienst (price DM 3.50). This calendar wants to bring joy on 365 days of the new year! Give this pleasure to your oriental neighbour and send us your order soon."

Ein Weihnachtsgeschenk

Haben Sie schon darüber nachgedacht, was Sie wohl Ihren moslemischen Nachbarn zu Weihnachten schenken können?
Wir empfehlen Ihnen den neuen biblischen Wandkalender für 1979. Er ist in Arabisch, Türkisch und Urdu beim Orientdienst erhältlich (Preis: DM 3,50).
Der Kalender will Freude bringen, an 365 Tagen des neuen Jahres! Machen Sie Ihrem orientalischen Nachbarn diese Freude und senden Sie uns Ihre Bestellungen bald.

```
TAKVİM

TÜRKÇE-ALMANCA
—
TÜRKISCH-DEUTSCHER

KALENDER
1979
```

كل عام
وأنتم بخير

١٩٧٩

V
THROUGH CHILDREN TO PARENTS: A SPECIAL MISSIONARY APPROACH

As early as 1972 a staff member of Orientdienst took some special interest in the children of Muslim immigrant labourers, and the annual report of the organization for that year states briefly:

"Mrs. Oezer gathered during the afternoons Turkish school children to watch them while they were doing their homework, to play with them and to tell them stories from the Bible. Doing this she succeeded in establishing good contacts with the parents of Turkish children ..." [1]

This kind of work resulted from the situation of Turkish children in Germany. In many cases both parents went out to work during the daytime and children, who had to attend school classes in the mornings, were left by themselves in the afternoons. The missionary organization arranged a room and a staff member who would look after these children, take care of them while the parents were out at work and also watch over their homework from school. At the same time the message of Jesus Christ was to be taught to the children.

This became a regular feature of the work of Orientdienst and was again included in the later annual reports:

"Mrs. Oezer did good work among the children of Turkish immigrant labourers. She took care of them in Wiesbaden during hours of doing homework and occupied them with handicrafts and games. She also made efforts to bring the message of Jesus Christ to them ..." [2]

---

1. *Nachrichten der Ev. Mission in Oberagypten*, Nr.6 (Dez. 1973), p.84; also No.6 (Dez. 1974) etc.
2. *Nachrichten der Ev. Mission in Oberagypten*, Nr.4 (August 1973), p.54.

The following recent brief report by one of the Orientdienst part-time staff may help to illustrate the aims and methods of child evangelism and door to door visits: "A week among Turks".

"I am the Lord, the God of all flesh; is anything impossible for me? (Jeremiah 32:27). This word of God is a great consolation for us working among Turks. For us it is a miracle and a sign for the greatness of our Lord that so far on every Saturday the number of Turkish children in our group has increased; however, not all of them are allowed to attend regularly. The aim of our work is to present the joyful message of Jesus to those children and also to their parents through the children. That needs much wisdom and understanding from the Lord. We often have problems to follow the way of thinking of the children. Our biggest problem is language. As to the biblical tales, the older children of about 9-12 years of age help in translating. This is, of course, not easy. The hymns we sing in Turkish, and here all children join in, even the small ones of four to five years of age. In fact, just those little ones proved already as 'little missionaries' when they sang the newly learnt songs innocently at home. When we bring the children back to their homes after the children's meeting, we do sometimes find opportunities to talk in some families. Cassettes with gospel lectures are of great help. Since the Turks are strongly rooted in their way of life influenced by Islam and tradition, and often have a completely wrong picture of Christianity, they are very reserved towards our faith, and sometimes suspicious. However, where we could establish some contacts and some trust had grown, they became open for the message of the Gospel. We were privileged to experience how God opened hearts and some individuals found their way to Jesus. To my great joy, there was a believing Turkish woman here in Brake during my period of stay. While my companions drove with their teams, to the places of their work, I stayed behind, to do a long awaited task. I have experienced: the Lord rewards hundredfold.

"During our visits Y and myself had a very beautiful togetherness and with the Lord. Y had left Islam about ten years ago for Christ. Her aim is to bring the Gospel to her countrymen. Her visit was a great encouragement for us as "turk-team" - for me it was an experience to visit other Turks together with someone who knew the language.

"During that period we visited about ten families. In some of the families we could read from the Bible, or tell tales to the Children, or give straightforward witness. In other families it was just renewal of contact.

"For us as a team, this mission brought a new insight. So far we thought that the strong opposition of some families against our work was due to the opening of a Quranic school which operates here in Lemgo since January 1978. However, we were mistaken. The opposition had come from German neighbours of the Turkish families. They meant to prevent the Turks from sending their children to our children's meetings. Please pray for those neighbours!" [3]

In either case, the missionaries were able to achieve two objectives in one go, namely:

- to work with and influence the children of Muslims; and
- to thus get acquainted with the parents of these children and try to bring their message to them.

The statement in the second of the reports referred to is very clear in this:

"... in fact just those little ones proved already as 'little missionaries' when they sang the newly learnt songs at home. When we bring the children back to their homes after the children's meeting, we do sometimes find opportunities to talk in some families ..."

---

3. From *Orientdienst Information* 52/1978, p.3.

This approach of reaching the parents through the children is perhaps something which should be taken note of. It seems that the missionary exploits the weak position of a minority group and approaches this group via its weakest and most vulnerable members, namely the children.

VI

ORIENTDIENST LITERATURE

Orientdienst publishes and distributes three kinds of literature for three different groups of readers, namely:

1. Literature for Christians meeting Muslims, in German.
2. Literature on mixed marriages between Christians (women) and Muslims (men), in German.
3. Biblical and other Christian literature for Muslims, in Turkish, Arabic, Persian, Urdu and German.

There are also some miscellaneous materials circulated by Orientdienst, such as some books for children, some entertaining literature and cassettes and tracts, mainly in Turkish.

1. Literature

Most prominent among literature for Christians meeting Muslims is the series "Christianity and Islam", which was begun in 1971 and contains some of the lectures and speeches given on the occasion of the annual assembly and training camp of Orientdienst. Below follows a brief description of the series, which will help in understanding the background from which Orientdienst wishes its staff to approach Islam.

(i) Christianity and Islam Books (Published on behalf of Orientdienst)

Book 1: *The Church in the Territory of Islam*, W. Hopfner, Wiesbaden 1971, 60pp.

Contents:

Preface, W. Hopfner

Introduction, Prof. J. Bouman

The situation of the church in pre-Islamic times, Dr. W. Hage; Umma and community, Dr. S. Raeder
The Coptic Church and Islam, W. Hopfner
Turkish Christians in Midiyat (South-East Turkey), W. Hopfner

Book 2: *History of Islam*, W. Hopfner, Wiesbaden 1971, 72pp.

Contents:

Preface
Tradition and Modernity in Islam, Prof. B. Spuler
Origin of Islam and its development as a community, J. Brugman
Development of Islam as religion and theology, J. Brugman
The medieval European church faced with Islam, Dr. S. Raeder

Book 3: *Belief in Islam*, W. Hopfner, Wiesbaden 1971, 60pp.

Contents:

Introduction, Dr. S. Raeder, Prof. H. Kraemer
Islamic and Christian concept of God, Dr. S. Raeder
The view of Jesus in the Quran, W. Hopfner
Abraham, the father of faith, in the Old Testament, Prof. N. Moritzen
Abraham in the Quran, Prof. N. Moritzen
Polemics against Jesus as the Son of God, Prof. W. Holsten
Polemics of the Muslims against Jesus as Son of God and the dogma of Trinity, Prof. W. Holsten

Book 4:   *Ethics in Islam,*   W. Hopfner, Wiesbaden 1971, 70pp.

Contents:

Bible workshop: good deeds in the perspective of the sermon on the mount, Prof. J. Bouman
Good deeds in Islam, Prof. J. Bouman
Islam in its crisis of today, D. Vander Meulen
Predestination and the cross, Prof. N. Moritzen
The position of women in Islam, W. Hopfner
Some books recommended for the study of Islam, W. Hopfner

Book 5:   *Prophethood in Bible and Qur'an,* W. Hopfner, Wiesbaden 1971, 54pp.

Contents:

The Prophethood of the Old Testament in its essential traits, Prof. H.W. Wolff
Prophethood in the Koran, Dr. S. Raeder
Sura 55: Creation and Judgement: Essay in interpretation and criticism, Dr. S. Raeder

Book 6:   *Tolerance and Absolute Claim,* W. Hopfner, Wiesbaden 1975, 93pp.

Contents:

Preface, W. Hopfner
Tolerance and the message of God in Islamic and Christian perspectives, Dr. S. Raeder
The peculiarity of the Arab-Islamic psyche, Prof. J. Bouman
The art to live as minority, Dr. K. Cragg
Interpretation of Islam by Kraemer and Cragg, Prof. D. Mulder
The Christian church in Turkey, Prof. I. Missir

The Christ of Qur'an in the view of Nicolaus of Cues, Dr. S. Raeder.

Book 7: *Mysticism in Islam*, W. Hopfner, Wiesbaden 1976, 102pp.

Contents:

Preface, W. Hopfner
Sufism (Islamic Mysticism), Prof. E. Douglas
Seeking God, Prof. H. Kohlbrugge
Love of God in Islamic and Christian Mysticism, Dr. S. Raeder

Book 8: *Fasting - Islamic or Protestant?* W. Hopfner, Wiesbaden 1977, 47pp.

Contents:

Introduction
Ramadan-Fasting in the factory, W. Hopfner
Fasting is Protestant, S. Kettling

Book 9: *Islam in Indonesia*, W. Hopfner, Wiesbaden 1978, 74pp.

Contents:

Preface, W. Hopfner
Islam in Indonesia, Dr. O. Schumann
Proclamation of the gospel in modern Indonesia, S. Marantika
Final conclusion, B. Bowerk

Book 10: *Certainty of Belief in Islam and the Gospel*, W. Hopfner, Wiesbaden 1978, 40pp.

Contents:

Preface
Certainty of belief in Islam, Bishop J. Christensen
Certainty of belief and understanding of Islam of Luther, Dr. S. Raeder
Certainty of belief in the Syrian-Jakobite Church, Prof. W. Hage

Separate from the series "Christianity and Islam," a number of other booklets have been published. Among them the following came into wider circulation:

(ii) *Islam as Post Christian Religion*, W. Hopfner, Wiesbaden 1971, 98pp.

(iii) *Bible and Quran in Dialogue*, Orientdienst, Wiesbaden n.d., 16pp.

(iv) *Eschatology and Judgement in Islamic and Christian Perspective*, Orientdienst, Wiesbaden, n.d., 23pp.

(v) *Suffering in Islamic Mysticism*, Orientdienst, Wiesbaden n.d., 23pp.

(vi) *The Coptic Church*, Orientdienst, Wiesbaden, n.d.

Also published and distributed by Orientdienst are the following two translations into German:

(vii) Brown, David: *Allah der Allmachtige, Jesus der Gekreuzigte? Die Frage nach dem Sinn des Kreuzes* (German translation of "The Cross of the Messiah") publ. by Orientdienst, Wiesbaden 1976, 96pp.

(viii) Dehqani-Tafti, Hassan: *Bild meiner Welt* (German translation of "Design of my world") publ. by Orientdienst, Wiesbaden 1976, 77pp.

The latter publication is written by a Persian convert to Christianity, who later in his life became a bishop of Tehran. The book has been translated into a number of other languages and is also distributed in Arabic.

2.   Literature on Mixed Marriages

In this field Orientdienst has published 7 booklets, one of them being a translation from English. All of these booklets aim at discouraging Christian women from marrying Muslims (and non-Europeans) by relating the experiences of some of the unfortunate women who did so. There are two basic ideas underlying these publications:

(a) The cultural differences between Germans and Muslims are too big to overcome easily, and Islam with its supposed disregard for women makes this an even more painful experience.

(b) A Germany woman marrying a Muslim would either become a Muslim herself, or would at least not be able to make her own children good Christians.

The titles of the booklets are as follows:

(i) *Christian-Islamic Mixed Marriages* (general)
(ii) *Marriage African Style?*
(iii) *To Become His Wife?* (Turkish situation)
(iv) *Marriage with Foreigners* Africa and Asia)
(v) *Marriage with Foreigners*
(vi) *The Women in Egypt Today*
(vii) *Temperament and Character of the Arabs* (select translation)

3.   Biblical and Other Christian Literature for Muslims

These include translations of the Gospel in Turkish and Arabic, gospel tracts in Turkish, Arabic and Persian and a number of books and pamphlets in Turkish and Arabic.

Among these books are:

(i) *Allahin Ozgurluk Savascilari*
(ii) *Dunyanin Sonu*
(iii) *Seytandan Kacisim*
(iv) (The Third Alternative)
(v) (The End of the World)
(vi) (The Life of Jesus)
(viii) (The Logic of Faith)
(viii) (Science is Lying)

For Children:

(ix) The Appletrees
(x) The Great Flood (Noah)
(xi) The Twelve Brothers (Joseph)

Orientdienst also distributes cassettes with gospel passages, explanations and music, and the evangelical newspaper YASAM printed in Turkish for reaching Turkish immigrants.

ISLAMIC FOUNDATION PUBLICATIONS ON STUDIES IN CHRISTIAN-MUSLIM RELATIONS

Study Papers

— Indonesia: A Survey of Christian Churches and Missions
— Indonesia: How Muslims are made Christians
— Christian Mission among Muslims in Bangladesh — A Survey
— Birth of Bangladesh — The Political Role of Missions
— The Henry Martyn Institute of Islamic Studies
— Christian Presence in Indonesia — A View of Christian-Muslim Relations

Situation Reports

— The Fulani Evangelisation Scheme in West Africa
— Indonesia: Government Decrees on Mission and Subsequent Developments
— Mission to Muslims in Germany: A Case Study of the "Orientdienst" the major mission organisation
— Christian Presence in the Gulf Region
— Christian Literature Crusade: Case Study of a Mission Organisation
— Christianity and Mission in Mali
— Christian Mission in Pakistan — A Survey

Documents

— Dialogue between Christians and Muslims.
   Part 1: Dialogue between Christians and Muslims: A Survey
   Part 2: Christian Guidelines for Dialogue with Muslims
   Part 3: Dialogue between Christians and Muslims — Statements and Resolutions
— Christian Mission and Islamic Da'wah — Conference Proceedings of 1976 Chambesy Dialogue

Christianity: A Series of Bibliographies

— A Select and Annotated Bibliography of General and Introductory Christian Books
— A Select and Annotated Bibliography of Christian Literature for Muslims in Current Usage for Mission among Muslims

Seminar Papers

— Christians in the Qur'ān and the Sunnah
— Some Reflections on Dialogue between Christians and Muslims